Roma caput mundi: there is no denying the sense of permanence and stability which nowadays attaches to the city of Rome and the Vatican in particular as the centre of the Western church. But this sense of Rome as an historical focal point is a relatively recent phenomenon: during the early 14th century, the papacy had moved to Avignon, and Rome from the religious point of view was an abandoned city. Then came years of confusion, with the appearance of various antipopes, leading to the Council of Constance in 1414. Other pretenders to the papal crown appeared and the *status quo* – a single pope resident in Rome – was not restored until the mid-15th century. Even then the situation was still deeply unstable, and the great days of late renaissance and baroque Rome could hardly have been the subject even of dreams. As late as 1527 Rome was sacked by imperial forces, and Pope Clement VII held prisoner for six months.

With the reign of Paul III (1534-49) the papacy took on a new stability, and the artistic life of the city could at last flourish. The great institutions which promoted music had been founded only in the years around 1500: Pope Sixtus IV (1471-84) gave the papal choir new creative motivation, and Pope Julius II founded a new group of musicians in 1513 to provide music for the Vatican Basilica, St Peter's. So the twin choirs, the Sistina and Giulia, came into being. The greater stability occasioned by the papal court settling in Rome meant that singers from both northern Europe and Iberia were attracted to work there. Not only could they obtain a prestigious position, but honorary church appointments might be bestowed upon them, guaranteeing their financial well-being on return home. It is only as the century progressed that Italian musicians eventually came to the fore and, in the wake of the achievement of Palestrina, began to dominate the music of the Roman basilicas and churches towards the end of the century.

In compiling a volume of motets by musicians associated with Rome, not all the composers are Italian, rather they reflect the international life of the city. Josquin Desprez came from the Low Countries and spent much of his career as a singer and composer in the Italian peninsula, including some years in the papal choir around 1490. Another Northerner, Jacques Arcadelt, sang in the papal choir for a decade from around 1540; he is best known for his madrigals, but his motet *Hodie beata virgo Maria* is one of a small number of sacred works, most of which reached publication in anthologies while he was still alive.

Two further foreigners, both Spanish, are represented. Cristóbal de Morales from Seville, who worked in the papal choir for a decade from 1535, forming part of the Spanish clique which continued for many decades from the time of the Spanish pope, Callistus III, almost a century earlier. His music is sadly neglected, despite the fact that it reached a very wide circle even during his own lifetime. The other Spaniard is Tomás Luis de Victoria, who spent his Roman years in the service of the Aragonese national church in Rome, as well as directing the music at one of the institutions spawned by the counter-reformation, the Collegium Germanicum for the formation of seminarians.

The earliest of the Italians included in this volume is Costanzo Festa, who was perhaps of Florentine extraction, and certainly belonged to the papal choir during the reign of the Medici pope, Leo X, probably assuming his responsibilities in 1517. Some of his motets can be taken as referring to political developments, including the sack of Rome. His music circulated widely; only Palestrina and Josquin can rival the number of his pieces which survive in the Sistina and Giulia archives. Palestrina tends to dominate any assessment of Roman renaissance church music, and not without some justification when one considers how much material can still be found in the archives of the city. He needs little introduction here, except to say that our appreciation of the quality of his music should not be eclipsed by the agonizing chore of studying his style, which has prevented generations of students from seeing him as a highly imaginative composer, rather than a source of counterpoint exercises. Luca Marenzio, a contemporary of Palestrina, never held a church appointment in Rome, rather he was active in the households of some leading ecclesiastical families, while accepting some church duties on a freelance basis.

It should come as no surprise to find that Roman composers began to write small-scale motets with continuo accompaniment in around 1600. The paired-down scoring matched the limited resources available to many churches, away from the major basilicas, where it was difficult to find and employ sufficient singers to perform traditional contrapuntal music in an adequate fashion. Within the first few years of the century Rome was as active as anywhere in Italy, including Venice, in the development of motets for few voices, and it is to this tradition of pragmatic church music that the works by Giovanni Francesco Anerio and Giovanni Bernardino Nanino belong. Their publications achieved a large number of reprints in the first decades of the new century, showing that such music was in wide demand for church use.

Performance

However greatly Palestrina was revered during his lifetime, new trends in Roman music emerged speedily after his death. The new generation were not so beholden to him as to continue slavishly to imitate his style, as some scholars have claimed. Palestrina's music, when seen from an historical perspective, is not quite what it may appear on the page: singers improvised freely over the long, flowing melodic lines; instruments would have performed with and replaced some of the voice parts; and the organ would often have provided a choral support to the texture. Because of this I have provided the Palestrina, Victoria and Marenzio motets with basso seguente parts, rather than a keyboard reduction for rehearsal. Except for *Amor Jesu dulcissime* and *Magnificat octavi toni*, which

require a keyboard continuo, all the motets may be performed unaccompanied.

The arrangement of the volume has followed the liturgical year through from Advent onwards, showing that this music (for all its aesthetic aspects) was practical in intent, and designed to adorn the liturgical celebration.

Sources

Source details are given at the top of each piece. Some pieces are edited from later sources in order to emphasize that the polyphonic tradition continued alongside newer styles through a wide geographical area. In view of the practical nature of the volume, one appropriate, reliable source for each piece has been selected, and therefore no cross-references are made to alternative readings.

Editorial method

Note values have generally been halved, and quartered in triple-time passages. Prefatory staves indicate original clefs, pitch and mensuration. Ditto marks in word underlay have been expanded without notice. Editorial accidentals are placed above the notes to which they apply. ⌐⌐ and ⌐ ¬ are used to indicate ligatures and coloration respectively in the source. Modern voice designations are editorial. All other editorial additions are placed in square brackets.

Graham Dixon
October 1994

Meisterwerke aus Rom

EINLEITUNG

Roma caput mundi (Rom ist das Haupt der Welt): Die Stadt Rom und insbesondere der Vatikan gelten heutzutage als das Zentrum der westlichen Kirche, das Beständigkeit und Stabilität ausstrahlt. Dieses Verständnis Roms als eines historischen Fixpunktes ist allerdings ein vergleichsweise neues Phänomen in der Geschichte: Während des frühen 14. Jahrhunderts verlagerte sich der Sitz des Papstes nach Avignon, und Rom war – aus religiöser Sicht – eine verlassene Stadt. Darauf folgten Jahre der Unruhen, in denen es immer wieder Gegenpäpste gab. Diese politischen Konstellationen führten 1414 zum Konstanzer Konzil. Auch nach dem Konzil gab es wiederum verschiedene Anwärter auf den päpstlichen Thron und der heutige status quo – ein einziger Papst mit Sitz in Rom – wurde erst Mitte des 15. Jahrhunderts wieder erreicht, allerdings immer noch von Instabilität gekennzeichnet. Die bedeutende Rolle, die Rom in der späten Renaissance und im frühen Barock zuwachsen sollte, konnte man damals wohl noch nicht einmal in den kühnsten Träumen vorhersehen. Noch im Jahre 1527 wurde Rom durch kaiserliche Truppen erobert (sacco di Roma) und Papst Clemens VII. sechs Monate als Gefangener gehalten.

Unter Papst Paul III. (1534-1549) stabilisierte sich die Herrschaft des Papstes, und das künsterlerische Leben in der Stadt konnte sich endlich ungestört entwickeln. Erst um das Jahr 1500 herum waren die großen Institutionen zur Förderung der Musik eingerichtet worden: Papst Sixtus IV. (1471-1484) gab der päpstlichen Kapelle neue künstlerische Inspiration. Papst Julius II. gründete 1513 ein neues Musik-Ensemble zur Musikpflege an der Balilika des Vatikans, S. Peter. Auf diese Weise gab es nebeneinander zwei Chöre, den Sixtinischen und den 'Julianischen', nämlich den des Petersdomes. Dadurch, daß sich der päpstliche Hof dauerhaft in Rom niederließ, wurden Sänger sowohl aus Nordeuropa wie auch von der iberischen Halbinsel angezogen. Sie konnten hier nicht nur eine angesehene Stellung erwerben, sondern auch ehrenhafte kirchliche Ämter erhalten, die ihnen finanzielle Sicherheit nach ihrer Rückkehr in die Heimatländer versprachen. Erst im Laufe des 16. Jahrhunderts dominierten die italienischen Musiker und begannen dann unter dem Einfluß der Errungenschaften Palestrinas die Musik der römischen Basiliken und Kirchen zum Ende des Jahrhunderts hin entscheidend zu prägen.

Bei der Zusammenstellung einer Sammlung von Motetten solcher Komponisten, die in Rom wirkten, ergibt es sich zwangsläufig, daß nicht alle Komponisten aus Italien stammen, sondern daß sie vielmehr das internationale Leben dieser Stadt widerspiegeln. Josquin Desprez kam aus den Niederlanden und verbrachte einen Großteil seines künstlerischen Lebens als Sänger und Komponist auf der italienischen Halbinsel, darunter auch einige Jahre um 1490 in der päpstlichen Kapelle. Ein anderer Musiker aus dem Norden, Jacques Arcadelt, sang um 1540 etwa eine Dekade lang in der päpstlichen Kapelle. Er ist am bekanntesten für seine Madrigale, aber zu seinen wenigen geistlichen Werken, von denen die meisten noch zu seinen Lebzeiten in Sammlungen publiziert wurden, gehört die Motette *Hodie beata virgo Maria*.

Zwei weitere Nicht-Italiener, beide aus Spanien, sind in unserer Sammlung vertreten. Cristóbal de Morales aus Sevilla sang ab 1535 für etwa zehn Jahre in der päpstlichen Kapelle. Er gehörte zu den Spaniern, die ihren Einfluß über viele Jahrzehnte hinweg am päpstlichen Hof wahrten, noch aus der Zeit des Spanischen Papstes, Callixtus III., herrührend, der fast ein Jahrhundert vorher geherrscht hatte. Seine Musik wird leider wenig aufgeführt, obwohl sie zu seiner Zeit weit verbreitet war. Der andere Spanier ist Tomás Luis de Victoria, der in Rom in den Diensten der Nationalkirche von Aragon stand. Außerdem leitete er das musikalische Leben an einem der Institute, deren Gründung auf die Gegen-Reformation zurückgeht, dem Collegium Germanicum, welches die Ausbildung von Seminaristen zum Inhalt hatte.

Der früheste in dieser Sammlung vertretene Italiener ist Costanzo Festa, der möglicherweise aus Florenz

stammte, und sicherlich während der Herrschaft des Medici-Papstes Leo X. zur päpstlichen Kapelle gehörte. Seine dienstlichen Verpflichtungen begannen wohl im Jahr 1517. Einige seiner Motetten lassen sich auf politische Ereignisse beziehen, unter anderem auch auf den sacco di Roma. Seine Werke waren weit verbreitet; nur Palestrina und Josquin können es mit ihm in der Anzahl von Werken aufnehmen, die in den Archiven der Sixtinischen Kapelle und des Petersdomes erhalten sind. Palestrinas Werke haben die Tendenz, jegliche Sammlung von Renaissance-Musik aus Rom zu beherrschen, nicht ganz ohne Grund, wenn man bedenkt, wieviel Material noch immer in den Archiven der Stadt zu finden ist. Er bedarf hier am wenigsten der Einführung, es sei aber doch die Bemerkung erlaubt, daß unsere Wertschätzung der Qualität seiner Musik nicht überschattet sein sollte durch die ermüdenden Untersuchungen seines Stils, die ganze Generationen von Studenten davon abhielten, ihn als einen höchst einfallsreichen Komponisten schätzen zu lernen und eben nicht nur als Quelle von Kontrapunkt-Übungen. Luca Marenzio, ein Zeitgenosse Palestrinas, hatte nie ein kirchliches Amt in Rom inne, sondern arbeitete bei einigen einflußreichen geistlichen Familien, während er gleichzeitig weitere kirchenmusikalische Aufgaben ohne feste Anstellung übernahm.

Daß die Komponisten in Rom um 1600 geringestimmige Motetten mit Continuo-Begleitung schrieben, überrascht nicht. Die kleinere Besetzung entsprach den begrenzten Möglichkeiten mancher Kirchen abseits der großen Basiliken, die Mühe hatten, genügend Sänger zu finden und einzustellen, die traditionelle kontrapunktische Musik befriedigend ausführen konnten. Innerhalb der ersten Jahre des neuen Jahrhunderts arbeitete man in Rom genauso wie anderswo in Italien, einschließlich Venedig, daran, Motetten für wenige Stimmen zu schreiben. Zu dieser Gattung von kirchlicher Gebrauchsmusik gehören die Werke von Giovanni Francesco Anerio und Giovanni Bernardino Na-nino. Ihre Publikationen wurden in den ersten Dezennien des 16. Jahrhunderts vielfach nachgedruckt, ein Hinweis darauf, wie beliebt diese Art liturgischer Gebrauchsmusik war.

Zur Aufführung

Ganz ungeachtet dessen, wie sehr Palestrina zu seinen Leb-zeiten verehrt wurde, entwickelten sich neue Tendenzen in der Kirchenmusik Roms doch sehr schnell nach seinem Tod. Die neue Komponistengeneration war nicht so sehr von ihm gefangengenommen, als daß sie seinen Stil sklavisch weitergeführt hätte, wie

einige Wissenschaftler behauptet haben. Die Musik Palestrinas sieht im historischen Kontext doch etwas anders aus, als sie auf dem Notenpapier erscheint: Sänger improvisierten über den langen, fließenden Melodielinien, Instrumente ergänzten, bzw. ersetzten einzelne Vokalstimmen und die Orgel gab sicher öfter dem gesamten Satzgefüge einen akkordischen Zusammenhalt. Aus diesem Grund habe ich für die Motetten von Palestrina, Victoria und Marenzio einen Basso seguente und nicht einen nur für die Probe gedachten Klavierauszug geschrieben. Außer *Amor Dulcissime* und *Magnificat octavi toni*, die eine Continuo-Begleitung durch ein Tasteninstrument brauchen, können alle Motetten ohne Begleitung aufgeführt werden.

Die Reihenfolge der Werke in diesem Band folgt dem mit Advent beginnenden Kirchenjahr, da diese Musik trotz all ihrer ästhetischen Dimensionen von ihrer Intention her praktisch und für den gottesdienstlichen Gebrauch bestimmt war.

Zu den Quellen

Angaben zur Quelle werden über jedem Stück mitgeteilt. Einige Werke sind aus späteren Quellen ediert worden, um zu zeigen, daß sich die Tradition mehrstimmiger Musik in einem weiten geographischen Gebiet neben neueren kompositorischen Stilen erhielt. Angesichts der Tatsache, daß es sich hier nicht um eine wissenschaftliche, sondern um eine Ausgabe für die musikalische Praxis handelt, wurde eine verläßliche Quelle für jedes Werk ausgesucht; auf Verweise zu anderen, abweichenden Lesarten wurde verzichtet.

Zur Edition

Die Werke wurden generell unter Verkürzung der Notenwerke auf die Hälfte, bei dreizeitigen Abschnitten unter Verkürzung der Notenwerte auf ein Viertel übertragen. Die vorangestellten Notensysteme geben die ursprüngliche Schlüsselung, Tonhöhe und Mensur wieder. Textwiederholungen, die in der Quelle mit einem *idem*-Zeichen notiert sind, wurden ohne entsprechenden Hinweis ausgeschrieben. Vom Herausgeber zugesetzte Akzidentien werden über die Note gesetzt, für die sie gelten. ⌐‾‾‾⌐ und ⌐ ‾⌐ werden benutzt, um auf Ligatur bzw. Kolorierung hinzuweisen. Alle anderen herausgeberischen Ergänzungen werden durch eckige Klammern gekennzeichnet.

Graham Dixon
Oktober 1994

Pastores dicite, quidnam vidistis?

Musica cum vocibus quatuor vulgo motecta cognominata
(Venice, 1546) RISM 1546/9

Cristóbal de Morales
(*c*.1500-1553)

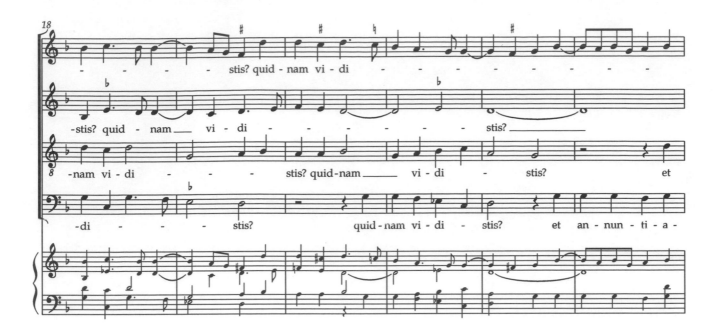

SECUNDA PARS

Magi viderunt stellam

Motecta … in omnibus solemn itatibus per totum annum,
concinuntur, noviter recognita, & impressa (Venice, 1603)

Tomás Luis de Victoria
(1548-1611)

Hodie beata virgo Maria

Tertius liber … Motteti del fiore
(Lyon, 1539) RISM 1539/10

Jacques Arcadelt
(?1505-1568)

12

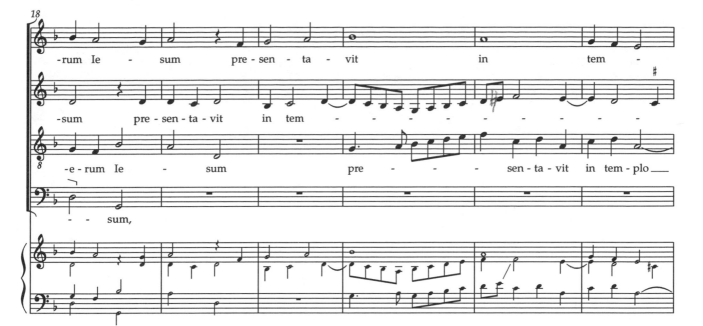

-rum Ie - sum pre - sen - ta - vit in tem -
-sum pre - sen - ta - vit in tem -
-e - rum Ie - sum pre - sen - ta - vit in tem - plo

- - sum,

-plo et Si - me - on re - ple - tus spi - ri - tu san - cto
-plo et Si - me - on re - ple - tus spi - ri - tu san - cto ac - ce - pit e -
et Si - me - on re - ple - tus spi - ri - tu san - cto ac - ce - pit e -
et Si - me - on re - ple - tus spi - ri - tu san - cto ac -

ac - ce - pit e - um in vul - nas su -
-um in vul - nas su - as, in vul - nas su -
- - um, ac - ce - pit e - um in vul - nas su -
-ce - pit e - um ac - ce - pit e - um in vul - nas su - as,

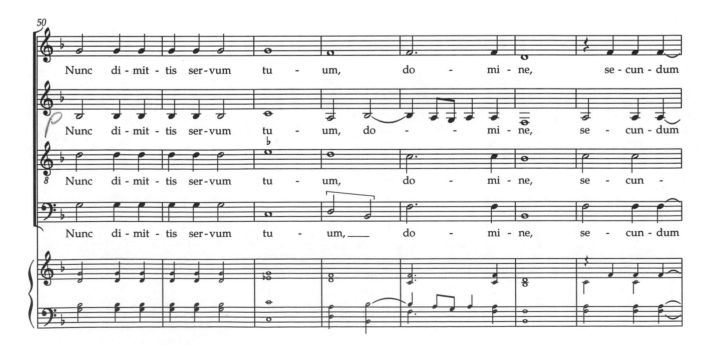

Jesus junxit se

Motecta festorum … liber primus
(Rome, 1622)

Giovanni Pierluigi da Palestrina
(c.1525-1594)

* Note omitted in source/ *Diese Note fehlt in der Quelle*

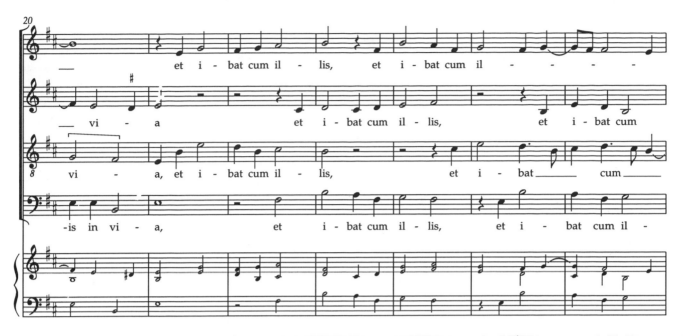

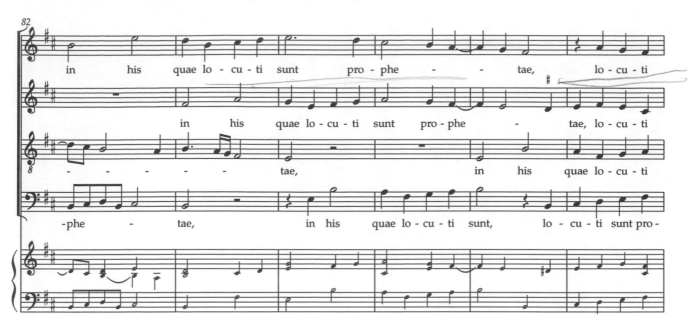

O Rex gloriae

Cantiones sacrae pro festis totius anni … quaternis vocibus
(Antwerp, 1603)

Luca Marenzio
(*c.*1553–1599)

Factus est repente

Biblioteca Apostolica Vaticana
MS Cappella Sistina 20, ff26v-28r

Costanzo Festa
(*c*.1490-1545)

* A in source/*A in der Quelle*

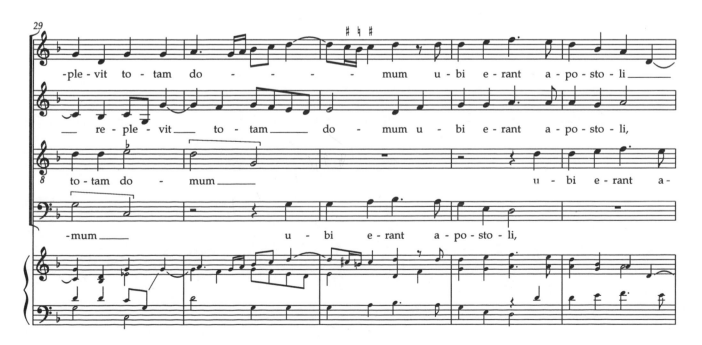

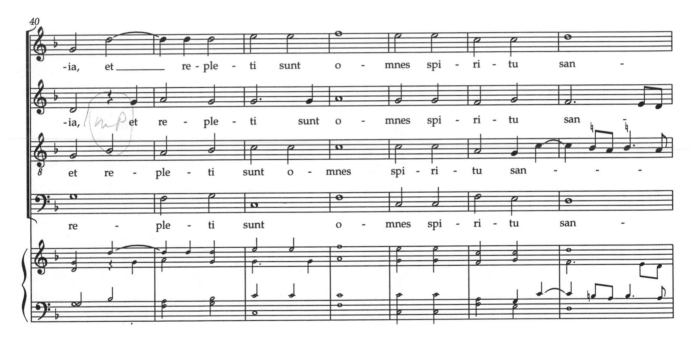

Jubilate Deo omnis terra

Tomus secundus psalmorum selectorum …
(Nuremburg, 1539) RISM 1539/9

Josquin Desprez
(*c*.1440-1521)

SECUNDA PARS

* G in source/*G in der Quelle*

Amor Jesu dulcissime

Motecta … binis, ternis, et quaternis vocibus …
(Rome, 1610)

Giovanni Bernardino Nanino
(*c.* 1560-1618)

Magnificat octavi toni (1614)

Psalmi vesperarum … cum basso ad organum
(Rome, 1614)

Giovanni Francesco Anerio
(*c*.1567-1630)

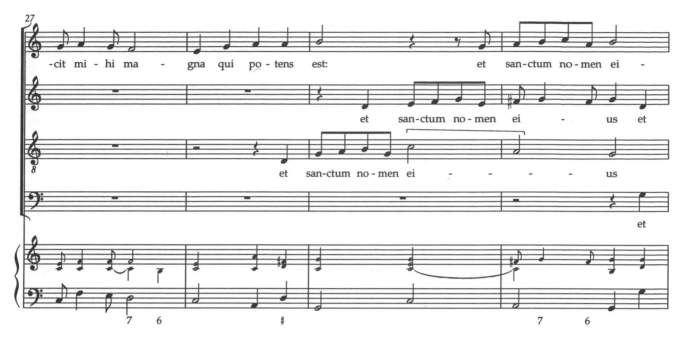

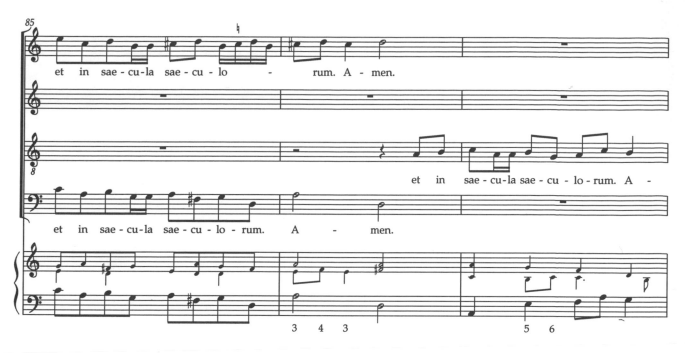

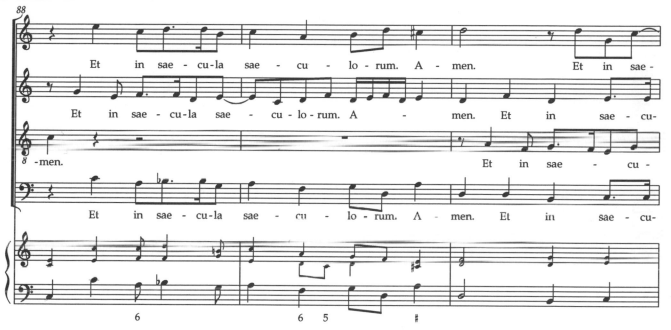

Translations

Pastores dicite, quidnam vidistis? (Christmas)

Shepherds, say what you saw, and announce the nativity of Christ. Noe, Noe.

Magi viderunt stellam (Epiphany)

The Magi saw the star, and said one to another 'This is the sign of a great king, let us go and find him, and offer him gifts of gold, frankincense and myrrh.' Alleluia.

Hodie beata virgo Maria (Candlemas)

Today the blessed Virgin Mary presented the child Jesus in the temple and Simeon, filled with the Holy Spirit, took him into his arms and blessed God, saying 'Now lettest thy servant depart in peace, O Lord, according to thy word'.

Jesus junxit se (Easter)

Jesus himself drew near to his disciples on the way and went with them. But their eyes were holden that they should not know him. And he said unto them, 'O fools and slow of heart to believe all that the prophets have spoken'. Alleluia.

O Rex gloriae (Ascension)

O King of Glory, and Lord of the Powers, who as victor didst ascend today above all the heavens, do not leave us orphans, but send unto us the promise of the Father, the Spirit of truth. Alleluia.

Factus est repente (Pentecost)

Suddenly there came a sound from heaven as of a rushing mighty wind. Alleluia. And it filled all the house where the apostles were. Alleluia. And they were all filled with the Holy Spirit and began to speak. Alleluia. The Spirit of the Lord hath filled the whole earth. Alleluia.

Jubilate Deo omnis terra (adapted from Psalm 99)

O be joyful in the Lord, all ye lands: serve the Lord with gladness, and come before his presence with exaltation. Know that the Lord is God: we are his people and the sheep of his pastures. O enter his gates with thanksgiving, and his courts with praise. *Second part*: Praise his name. The Lord is good; his mercy is eternal, and his truth from generation to generation.

Amor Jesu dulcissime

Most sweet love of Jesus, who are the glory of the blessed and the joy of the angels in the heavens. You gave yourself to be our food and the nourishment of travellers. Who has ever seen, who has ever heard of such things? Wonder all of you, that very God is become man!

Magnificat octavi toni

My soul doth magnify the Lord and my spirit hath rejoiced in God my Saviour. For he hath regarded the lowliness of his handmaiden. For behold from henceforth all generations shall call me blessed. For he that is mighty hath magnified me and holy is his name. And his mercy is on them that fear him throughout all generations. He hath shewed strength with his arm: he hath scattered the proud in the imagination of their hearts. He hath put down the mighty from their seat and hath exalted the humble and meek. He hath filled the hungry with good things and the rich he hath sent empty away. He remembering his mercy hath holpen his servant Israel as he promised to our forefathers, Abraham and his seed for ever. Glory be to the Father and to the Son and to the Holy Spirit, as it was in the beginning, is now, and ever shall be, world without end. Amen.

FABER MOTET SERIES

Each volume in the *Faber Motet Series* brings together the foremost composers working at a major musical city in the 16th and 17th centuries.

Rome, centre of the Western Church and a focus of musical excellence in the renaissance, played host to many of the leading church composers of the day, including Victoria, Josquin and Palestrina.

Jeder Band der *Faber Motet Series* stellt die bedeutendsten Komponisten vor, die in wichtigen Musikstädten des 16. und 17. Jahrhunderts gewirkt haben.

Die Stadt Rom, Mittelpunkt der Kirche im Abendland und Zentrum musikalischer Kunst während der Renaissance, war für viele führende Kirchenkomponisten ihrer Zeit, darunter Victoria, Josquin und Palestrina, musikalische Heimat.

Faber Motet Series:

Masterworks from Rome (ed. Dixon)
0 571 51260 7

Masterworks from Venice (ed. Roche)
0 571 51286 0

Faber Choral Programme Series:

This highly-acclaimed repertoire series for both mixed- and upper-voice choirs offers a wealth of fresh material from the 18th, 19th and 20th centuries in new editions representing superb value for money.

Currently includes works by Purcell, Schubert, Schumann, Mendelssohn, Bruckner, Dvořák, Verdi, Debussy, Fauré, Saint-Saëns, Stanford, Parry, Holst, Bridge, Warlock, Gilbert & Sullivan, Britten and Vaughan Williams, as well as arrangements of folksongs and show tune hits. For further details contact your local music shop, or Faber Music at the address below.

ISBN 0-57

FABER MUSIC · 3 QUEEN SQUARE · LONDON

9 780571 512607